ABANDONED PENNSYLVANIA

JANINE PENDLETON

FONTHILL

A journey is not measured in miles travelled; it is measured by the memories you forge with your fellow travelers.

Fonthill Media Inc.
www.fonthillmedia.com
office@fonthillmedia.com

First published 2019

ISBN 978-1-63499-195-7

Typeset in Trade Gothic 10pt on 15pt
Printed and bound in England

CONTENTS

INTRODUCTION

"Virtue, Liberty and Independence" is the motto of the Keystone State of Pennsylvania.

The state has a central place in the history of the country. Not only was it one of the twelve original founding members of the United States, but the Declaration of Independence and the Constitution were both drafted in Philadelphia's Liberty Hall. The state was also central to the country's economic development; its two largest cities, Philadelphia and Pittsburgh, have a rich industrial history dating back over two centuries.

American industrialization was catalyzed in the early 1800s as Britain cut off essential supply lines during the War of 1812. The country looked inward to the dense forests (as a source of wood for the logging companies) and the abundant and thick coal seams (that provided a constant source of fuel). Coal was extensively mined in the areas surrounding Pittsburgh, as well as to the north east of Harrisburg. Mining and logging towns grew up all over Pennsylvania as America hungered for fuel to feed its fledgling iron, brass, tin, and glass industries

At the start of the twentieth century, Pennsylvania was an up-and-coming hive of industrial activity. Large steel companies were established in the major cities, and populations began to swell as immigrants from Europe flocked to the area. African Americans migrated from the rural south, joining the already large workforce. The promise of fair wages for a hard day's work was certainly an attractive proposition. World War II created a pressing need for American-made steel, and the factories operated twenty-four hours a day to keep up with the soaring demand.

From the mid-1970s to the 1980s, the bubble burst. In one decade, industry collapsed and over half the state's steel jobs disappeared. The generally accepted cause was the oil embargos from the Middle East triggering the "oil shock" and a corresponding economic downturn. The consumer demand for steel products declined, and the steel manufacturers were forced to cut production and lower retail prices to unprofitable levels. There were mass layoffs of the working-class union jobs, as one by one, the steel mills closed. Thousands were left jobless with families to feed and little prospect of putting food on the table.

Predictably, there was a mass flight of the former workforce and their families over the following years. They left the major cities in droves in search of work elsewhere, leaving many buildings and services redundant. When the Great Recession hit in the late 2000s, there was further migration out of the industrial cities and another period when buildings and facilities were left abandoned.

After these two mass exoduses, a wealth of infrastructure was rendered obsolete. The cities of Pennsylvania are littered with abandoned churches, discarded as the small, scattered congregations merged together. Schools and hospitals closed down and were left to rot as the number of students and patients shrank to unsustainable sizes.

Other buildings have simply become casualties of changing trends and tastes over the decades. There are forgotten theaters, which once hosted sell-out performances but now lie silent and lost. As IMAX and Netflix evolved, these old screens and stages failed to complete. Old theme parks closed as their rides aged and the excitement they offered waned. Transport technology constantly marches forward and the outdated relics are left behind; trolley cars from the 1950s and steam locomotives lie rusting and disused.

One by one, these hidden treasures are lost as time and the world moves on around them. Some are renovated, restored to their former glory or tastefully converted to other uses while retaining many original features. However, for every building saved, there are countless others that meet a more tragic fate. Whether the buildings merely collapse as they succumb to the ravages of time or are purposely destroyed by official demolition (or unofficial arson attacks), the result is the same. The loss of history is something that always comes with a measure of sadness.

This book explores the beauty that lies in these forgotten places, often hiding in plain site on the streets of Pennsylvania.

1

FALLEN IDOLS

Tabernacle Baptist Church

The Tabernacle Baptist Church was built around 1905. Originally a Presbyterian Church, it changed denomination sometime in the 1970s. The congregation was later forced to relocate as the roof began to buckle and collapse. This impressive building has been left to rot for years.

The building was designed by a once-prominent local architect, who, a few short years beforehand, had won a large government contract to design the State Capitol building. Only a few years after the church was built, he was convicted of "graft"—buying building materials for the Capitol building from very specific third parties at highly inflated prices, meaning government funds were misdirected for personal gain. The state investigation team became suspicious when the total cost of the project came out at nearly triple the originally approved budget. Along with four others, he was convicted of corruption and imprisoned for two years.

Nowadays, the church is filled with pigeons, and piles of rubble and rubbish lie scattered everywhere. The stairs and floor are collapsing in several areas of the sanctuary. Most of the windows have been smashed and boarded up in a slapdash fashion.

Built around 1905, this church has been left to crumble due to structural safety concerns.

The Tabernacle Baptist Church has become a dumping ground for rubbish and unwanted items.

Gothic Revival Church

This Gothic-Revival style Roman Catholic church was constructed in the 1840s and has now been abandoned for over twenty years. It is the oldest surviving example of the several hundred churches designed and built by a world-renowned American ecclesiastical architect. Substantial renovation work was undertaken at the end of the nineteenth century, but most of the original features remain intact. For the local community, the building remains a beautiful and cherished part of the urban landscape. Over two decades of graffiti plaster the walls, but seemingly even this flagrant vandalism fails to dull the charm of this building.

As well as being architecturally stunning, this historic building has links to two Catholic saints. However, that has not saved it and it is currently in very poor condition, requiring millions of dollars to renovate. The church passed ownership from the city's diocese some years ago and is now owned by a local non-profit wellness group. They purchased the site to level the church and build a new facility.

A preservation order saved it, but the church has been living on a knife edge for the last ten years, alternating between preservation order protection and demolition grant. Local preservationists then appeal the demolition order and the cycle beings anew. The future remains uncertain for this grand building.

Inside the church, the nave is two stories tall with a balcony level above the triple entrance vestibule. The central aisle is lined with ornate columns, supporting dramatic, pointed Gothic arches. Six skylights illuminate the church, which can be seen through the collapsing ceiling above the main chamber. Light also pours in from the lancet windows flanking the nave. At the far end of the church, in the sanctuary, there are three beautiful stained-glass windows above the tall marble altar, which both date to the end of the nineteenth century.

This nineteenth-century Gothic-Revival style Roman Catholic church has been abandoned for over twenty years.

Graffiti now plasters the walls of this grand building.

Above the tall marble altar, there are three beautiful stained-glass windows.

Blue Church and Parish School

The Blue Church and Parish School lie abandoned in a waterfront neighborhood of a large Pennsylvanian city. The church has been closed for around five years; the schoolhouse had been vacated and left to decay for a decade prior to this. As well as the church and schoolhouse, there is a convent and rectory in other buildings.

A large German population moved to this area in the mid-1800s, lured by the prospect of jobs and a new way of life. Several up-and-coming industrial plants had been established here. Two decades later the German population had expanded and was now thriving. The Protestants set up a reformed church, whereas the Roman Catholics founded this sanctuary. The church cornerstone indicates that this brownstone-clad building was completed in the 1890s. Services were held here for nearly 120 years, in the latter years serving the large Polish community that continues to live in the surrounding neighborhoods.

The church is in almost pristine condition, complete with an impressively large marble altar as well as a pipe organ. The tall vaulted ceiling is painted cornflower blue and bright yellow. Large hexagonal pendant lights hang along the midline of the room. The walls would have originally had marble or stone tablets inset into them, which would have borne carvings of psalms or prayers. These have been removed, sadly. Above the column-supported arches lining the church aisles are paintings of saints or other religious figures embellished with halos.

The adjacent schoolhouse opened in the 1920s. There are brightly painted passageways and a performance hall with a stage. The classrooms are small and simple, traditional and functional. The school has been abandoned for a decade longer than the church, although signs of damp and decay are still relatively minor. Children's drawings still hang from a piece of string across the blackboard where they were hung over fifteen years ago.

These buildings have now been sold, and plans approved for their re-purposing. The church will be converted into commercial space, including a large ground floor restaurant. The other buildings will be converted into living spaces.

This beautiful church has been closed for half a decade.

German migrant workers founded this Roman Catholic sanctuary in the mid-1800s.

The tall vaulted ceiling of this church is painted cornflower blue and bright yellow.

This place of worship served the local community for nearly 120 years.

The stunning pipe organ still resides here; it is in almost immaculate condition.

Sheet music and religious texts litter the floor surrounding the pipe organ.

This blue performance hall is in the adjacent schoolhouse. This school was opened in the 1920s.

The classrooms are small and functional. Children's drawings still hang from a piece of string in front of the blackboard.

The large teacher's desk faces the classroom; the central drawer is slighting ajar. Now, the desk only looks out across a sea of empty desks instead of pupils.

Many of the desks and chairs are neatly stacked up against the walls.

The main corridor has brightly colored pink walls. Several classrooms lead off from this hallway as well as numerous cupboards and storerooms.

These vintage child's chairs can be found in nearly every room, lining the sides of classrooms or neatly stacked in clusters.

HOLY CITY CHURCH

The Holy City Church was built just after the turn of the twentieth century in a Romanesque style. At the time, this small township had over twenty churches and a strong religious community, earning it the name "Holy City".

An auditorium was added five years after the church was constructed, and an educational building was added as a southern wing in the late 1920s. By the 1940s, the church was at its peak as a vibrant and bustling religious center. The congregation was 2,000 strong, and despite there being so many churches in the area, this church thrived.

As the twenty-first century arrived, the town's economy and demographics shifted in response to the decline in manufacturing industries. Affluent families left the town in droves, and the population that remained were mainly low-income families and senior citizens. The congregation was now a mere twenty-five people for Sunday service, usually the busiest time. The church diversified and became an emergency food bank, youth health center, and a senior care center. By the mid-2000s, the church and related services were set to close, amid low attendance and high heating bills.

A recovering alcoholic, now turned Baptist minister, arrived on the scene at the last minute with $700,000 to purchase the church. It seemed a miracle. He had visions of regenerating the church, including opening a public café and emergency shelter. The charitable organization he headed owned eleven properties, worth in excess of $4 million in total.

Alas, salvation was not at hand. After several years, the non-profit organization was in financial trouble. They owed over $2,000 in outstanding bills and unpaid taxes, and the IRS revoked their non-profit status (and the tax breaks that went with it). Many of the organization's buildings were shuttered and left vacant; this church is one of those causalities.

Left: The Holy City Church features Romanesque architecture. It was built in the early twentieth century.

Below: Shifting economics and demographics led to the abandonment of this church in the mid-2000s.

Church of Little Italy

The Church of Little Italy was built in the early 1900s, replacing an earlier church that was destroyed by a fire. The building is Baroque in style, sporting a triple-domed roof that was supported internally by Corinthian columns.

This area was originally settled by German immigrants in the nineteenth century, who migrated to the area to work in the fledgling steel industries. By the early 1900s, Italians and Sicilians were the dominant ethic groups of this area, which became known as "Little Italy." The church played a key role in the community, putting on sporting events for neighborhood children. During the 1940s and 1950s, the church would hold 1,000 worshippers in the nave and balcony. Officially, the church witnessed nearly 3,000 marriages and over 13,000 baptisms during the first half century of operation.

The congregations shrank. The Diocese was forced to close the church in the early 1990s, merging the dwindling congregations into another church elsewhere. The church lay unused for several years, before being bought by an independent non-denominational church group. After little more than a decade, the mounting repair and maintenance costs forced the group to vacate the church and put it back on the market. Sadly, no buyer has been found, and every year, the church crumbles and declines a little more.

The Baroque-styled Church of Little Italy features a domed roof, supported by Corinthian columns.

Dark Dogma Church

The Dark Dogma Church is over 120 years old; it has been abandoned for twenty of those years. The church was built in an imposing Gothic architectural style, with a tall looming vaulted ceiling. The hall is lined with brightly colored stained-glass windows, imported from Germany and made by the finest craftsmen of the time.

The old convent was converted into a girl's school at the turn of the twentieth century. The school taught practical skills such as cooking and dressmaking, as well as arts such as painting and music. The church was struck by lightning a few years later, starting a fire that destroyed almost everything. Yet the building was repaired and rose from the ashes.

The church closed in the early 1990s, as the number of parishioners dwindled. This decline was due to the mass exodus of the local population in response to closure of the steel mills, which were one of the main employers in this city. This church merged with five other churches in the area to form a new congregation at another premises.

In the mid-1990s, a non-denominational church purchased the building and the old school for less than $100,000. Full repairs were estimated to potentially cost up to $5 million to fully restore the building. They planned to turn the site into a charter school, but seemingly, these plans have evaporated. Repeated break-ins and ransacking by burglars mean the church is now a cavernous, empty void. Many items were taken over state lines and sold on the antiques black market and via auction houses; customers likely unknowingly receiving stolen property.

The owners let the empty church fall into neglect, losing interest in replacing boards that would only be torn off again. The church is now in a rundown and dilapidated state, covered with garish graffiti and tags. Scenes from the cult 1998 movie *Dogma* were filmed here.

Above: The imposing vaulted ceiling is a marvelous example of Gothic architecture.

Below: The Dark Dogma Church has been abandoned for twenty years. The building is over 120 years old.

The Blue Synagogue

When the Jewish community first began to settle here, religious services were held in homes and small rented halls. In the 1910s, congregations were founded as the population grew. By the 1920s, the community raised the money to build this synagogue as a hub for this flourishing area.

The walls of the main chamber are yellow, with the back wall lined with arches and stained-glass windows. The ceiling is painted a navy blue, with gilded, golden stenciling. The roof is supported by a large arch that cuts across the middle of the sanctuary, with a pendant light fitting hanging from the apex.

The beautiful circular sanctuary held over 1,000 worshippers and supported the community as it grew to its peak in the 1930s and 1940s. A decade later, a community center, chapel, and social hall were added. There was a Sunday school, nursery, and classrooms, where children were taught Hebrew. Every summer, a grand fundraiser was held on the grassy land around the synagogue; this was the annual highlight of the social calendar and the whole community would attend.

Declining industry and failed urban regeneration plans in the 1960s saw the area begin to decline. The Jewish community decreased in the 1970s, and the congregation began to dissipate as families moved to more suburban areas. It became clear to the congregational leadership that downsizing and relocation would be essential. The synagogue closed in the mid-1990s; the by now tiny congregation dwarfed by the large grand sanctuary. The beautiful wooden ark and Torah scrolls were moved into storage for safe keeping.

After forty years of economic slump, the area is showing a glimmer of hope. Trendy companies, boutique hotels, and popular restaurants are locating here. It seems that the future is looking brighter for this suburb. The synagogue, along with its 3.5-acre plot of land, is for sale for $1,750,000.

The Blue Synagogue was founded by a fledgling Jewish community in the 1920s.

The ornate navy-blue ceiling features gilded golden stenciling.

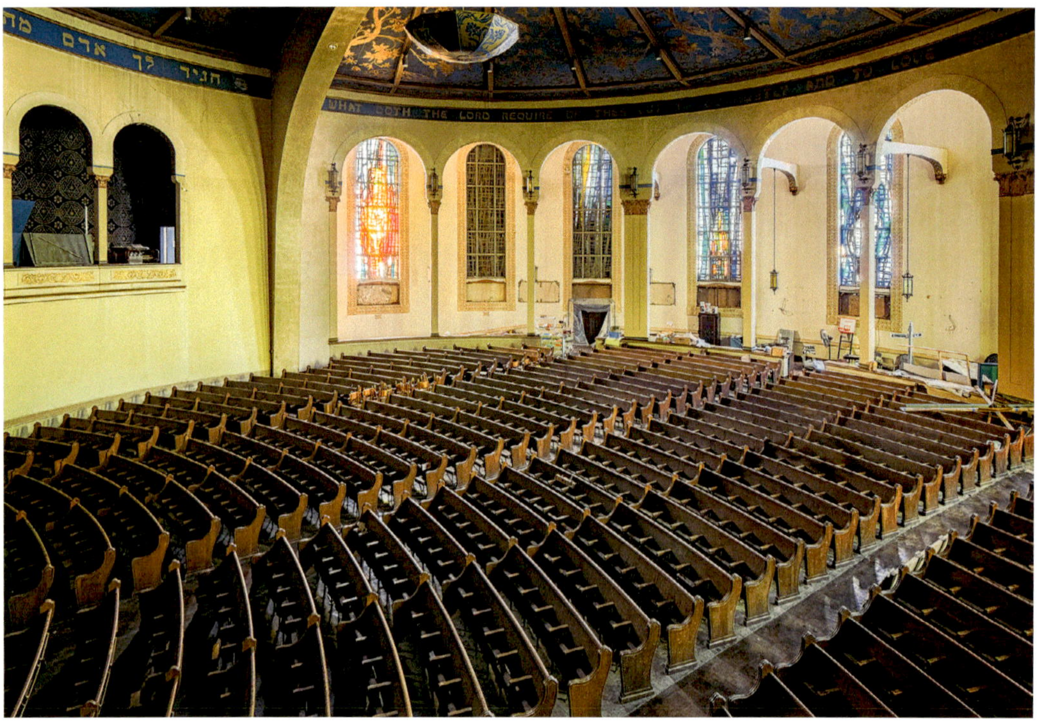

The community reached its peak in the 1930s and 1940s. At this time, the great circular chamber was filled with worshippers during services.

The congregation began to dissipate in the 1970s. Families began to move out of the city to start new lives in more suburban areas.

The tiny remaining congregation no longer require such a large synagogue, and it finally closed in the mid-1990s

2

FAILED BY THE SYSTEM

Eastern State Penitentiary

Eastern State Penitentiary began operations in 1829 and closed its doors in 1971. It then lay abandoned for over a decade, home only to stray cats and encroaching vegetation. In 1994, the building was opened for historical public tours. Built of austere local schist and gneiss metamorphic rock, the building stands on an 11-acre site, which is completely enclosed by a 30-foot tall perimeter wall and watched over by turreted guard towers. The administration building to the south of the prison was built in an imposing Gothic Revival architectural style and is the only entrance and exit.

Eastern State was proud to be the world's first true penitentiary, where inmates were expected to feel regret for their crimes. Initially incarcerated in individual cells, prisoners had plenty of time for quiet contemplation. Every day, the warden would visit each inmate to better evaluate their penitence and rehabilitation.

The original building design was set to have seven one-story cell blocks, fanning outwards from a central hexagonal rotunda like the spokes of a wheel. The central hub area allowed wardens to easily observe each of the cell corridors. By the time Cell Block 3 was built, the prison was well over capacity, and all subsequent cell blocks were built with two stories. When the prison finally closed, there were fifteen cell blocks, many hastily built in an attempt to ease the overcrowding. Of all the vaulted corridors, Cell Block 7 is unique. With a well-lit 30-foot high vaulted ceiling, this is the brightest cell block, with an almost cathedral-like atmosphere.

In the late 1800s, a state-of-the-art hospital was added to the site. Occupying Cell Block 3, it comprised operating theatres, laboratories, a pharmacy, x-ray rooms, hydrotherapy rooms, psychiatric department, and a solarium.

Diseases spread quickly through the cramped and crowded cell blocks and tuberculosis was a persistent threat. In the days before pharmaceutical cures for the disease had been discovered, fresh air and sunlight were the only treatments doctors could offer for this debilitating disease. Patients were able to get fresh, clean air in the outdoor exercise yards, but even so, half of all deaths (around 1,400) within the Penitentiary were tuberculosis related.

In 1929, the infamous gangster Alphonse "Scarface" Capone was arrested outside a movie theatre for carrying a concealed and unlicensed revolver. Handed a one-year sentence, he served eight months in a small cell in Eastern State. His cell has been recreated so visitors can get a sense of what it was like at the time. Local newspapers reported Capone enjoying many luxuries during his incarceration. His cell was reportedly plush with decorations that included oil paintings and large oriental rugs. He also is said to have spent hours listening to waltzes on a cabinet radio.

Eastern State Penitentiary operated between 1829 and 1971. The penitentiary was opened to the public for historical tours in 1994.

Inmates were incarcerated in separate cells, allowing them much time for quiet contemplation of their crimes. Every day, the warden would visit them here to evaluate their rehabilitation.

Eastern State was the world's first true penitentiary. The focus was on the rehabilitation of inmates, rather than merely using incarceration a punishment.

In 1929, the infamous gangster Alphonse "Scarface" Capone served eight months in a small cell at East State Penitentiary. This recreation of his cell shows what it would have looked like in the 1920s.

The original building design was set to have seven one-story cell blocks. These blocks radiate from a central hexagonal rotunda like the spokes of a wheel.

When the prison finally closed in 1971, there were fifteen cell blocks in total. Many of these were hastily built in an attempt to ease the overcrowding over the decades.

Cell Block 7 is unique. This is the brightest cell block, with an airy 30-foot high vaulted ceiling.

Some of the cells are used to display interesting original features, such as this dentist's chair in Cell Block 9.

In the late 1800s, a state-of-the-art hospital was added to the site, occupying Cell Block 3.

An old iron gate separates the medical wing from the central hub. The original red paint can still be seen on this decorative cross, flaking away as the decades pass by.

Inmates suffering from infectious diseases, such as tuberculosis, were quarantined in these single-bed wards.

The medical wing had dedicated rooms for treatment of inmates. This was once the door to the physiotherapy room.

Most of the medical equipment has been removed. One dimly lit room hides an original operating theatre lamp, tucked away in the corner.

Above left: Some of the older cell blocks are in an advanced state of decay. These areas are not part of the designated tour area.

Above right: Cell Block 9 houses displays and artifacts, such as old metal beds and a dentist chair. The cleanliness of this corridor is in start contrast to the older cell blocks.

ROTUNDA TOWN HALL

The Rotunda Town Hall is an old government building that was once a symbol of this town's independence from the larger city that now incorporates it. This incarnation of the town hall was built in the 1920s, in a Classical Revival architecture style. The building has been disused since the late 1990s, and estimates suggest it would take $10–15 million to renovate this lost place into flats. For the meantime, this dilapidated building awaits rejuvenation.

The first town hall was built on this site in the middle of the nineteenth century when the town was an independent municipality, before it was consolidated into the neighboring city some years later. Despite being known as "the Town Hall", the building has never truly served in this capacity. Over the early decades, it was used as a police station, and during the Civil War as a hospital. The original building was later declared structurally unsound and was demolished in the 1920s.

A few years later, the new town hall was constructed. The building covers 20,000 square feet over three floors. The clock and bell from the old town hall were lovingly re-instated in their new home atop the new tower. Below the clock tower, a green-painted rotunda was added. Two marble memorial tablets line the walls beneath the dome, emblazoned with the names of the town's fallen World War I soldiers.

Leading from the dome are corridors lined with various offices, now mostly empty. One office retains many interesting, original vintage signs that declare the room is the "Mayor's Office of Community Services." There are files and stationery littering the desk and the room appears relatively untouched, in stark contrast to the rest of the building.

The first town hall was built on this site in the middle of the nineteenth century. The original building was later declared structurally unsound and was demolished in the 1920s.

This incarnation of the town hall was built in a Classical Revival architecture style. Below the clock tower, there is a green-painted rotunda.

The corridors that lead off from the rotunda are lined with mostly empty offices. This one has a vintage sign indicating it was the "Mayor's Office of Community Services."

This Community Services office appears relatively untouched, in stark contrast to the rest of the building.

Flanking the main entrance is a pair of World War I memorial tablets. These marble slabs are etched with the names of the town's fallen soldiers.

The building has been disused since the late 1990s. Estimates suggest renovation work would cost over $10 million.

State Hospital for Women

The State Hospital for Women was built in the 1910s. It was initially founded as a village for "feeble-minded" woman, including teenagers. What was then termed "feeble-minded" would today encompass cognitive and neurophysiological disabilities, as well as other general learning disabilities. Initially, the institute housed around thirty-five residents in a single cottage. Over the next decade, prior to the Great Depression, six more cottages were constructed on the 220-acre site, allowing 500 patients to be treated there. Eventually, over 700 female residents lived and were treated in this isolated retreat.

The community was self-sufficient and included a fully working farm where food was grown for staff and residents. This formed part of the education and training of the women, which aimed to prepare them for work in the domestic sector or agriculture. The accepted medical theories for treating learning disabilities and mental health at that time were repetitive daily tasks in plain surroundings. Isolation from the community was also a commonly prescribed treatment, which explains the hospital's remote location.

In the 1960s, male patients were admitted for the first time, and the facility became recognized as a fully-fledged hospital, treating all types of mental and physical disabilities. By the 1960s, the facility had become the largest employer in the township with over 500 people working there. The hospital closed in the late 1990s due to changing economic factors at the state level, and the 200 remaining patients were relocated to other facilities. Some buildings have been brought back into use in recent years by the new landowners. There are also plans filed to turn the former mental institution into a resort and conference center. A championship-length golf course, indoor pool, health spa, and at least two restaurants are planned. The cottages that were once residence for mentally handicapped women will become condominiums and corporate accommodation.

The State Hospital for Women was founded to treat cognitive, neurophysiological and learning disabilities in the women of Pennsylvania.

These hospital wards have lay abandoned in disused since the late 1990s.

Right: The on-site mortuary would have stored the deceased until an autopsy could be performed. It was likely a mandatory requirement to ascertain the cause of death in the event of patient mortality.

Below: Most of the medical equipment and furniture has been removed since the hospital closed. Several rooms with baths and lifting equipment remain on the upper floors, but there is little real medical paraphernalia remaining.

During the early 1900s, those that suffered from maladies of the mind were isolated from the rest of society. Hospital, such as this one, were therefore typically built in remote locations.

The long corridors of the ground floor still smell of disinfectant, despite being abandoned over twenty years ago.

The remains of the morgue lay tucked away in an unassuming room. The body trays still rest inside these old cadaver fridges.

Over the decades, the hospital was expanded in several phases as new facilities and accommodation were added. Initially, only thirty-five resident patients could be treated in the original cottage.

As the hospital expanded, over 700 female residents lived and were treated in this isolated retreat. The hospital formed a self-contained community, with many amenities located on-site.

The most impressive building is the large auditorium. A silver star hangs above the stage, possibly a relic from one of the final performances. The ceiling is beginning to collapse, and rainwater cascades through during inclement weather.

An old autoclave is one of the only medical machines left; likely, it was deemed too much trouble to remove for sale or relocation.

The hospital remained a "women's retreat" for some fifty years. In the 1960s, male patients were admitted for the first time.

In recent years, plans have been filed to turn the former mental institution into a resort and conference center. The residential cottages will be converted to condominiums and corporate accommodation.

As you stand on the stage of the auditorium, the impressive size of the space can be appreciated. The ceiling is a haphazard mosaic of white tiles, which are interspersed with brown gaps where their counterparts have fallen over the years.

Above left: The old wooden benches of the auditorium are still in beautiful condition, covered in a layer of dust for decades of disuse.

Above right: Three octagonal Art Deco ceiling lights would have lighted the auditorium. During the day, natural light streams in through the large windows flanking the hall.

Below: The auditorium will hopefully be salvaged, in some fashion, when this site is converted to a resort and conference center over the next few years.

3

DECAYING ENTERTAINMENT

Blue Boxing Ring

The Blue Boxing Ring was a famous sports venue in the United States. Numerous sports magazines and commentators herald this prestigious arena as "the last great boxing venue" and "the number-one boxing venue in the world." It opened in the early 1960s but now lies unused, quietly decaying behind locked doors. The hot halogen lights still have power, and with a flick of the switch, some of the atmosphere of this spectacular place can be restored. The ground floor would have been packed tightly with stools and folding chairs on fight night, and spectators would eagerly lean over the guard rails on the upper tier seating to get closer to the action.

Originally, the three-storey building was apartments for *nouveau riche* businessmen. It was taken over in the 1920s by a fraternal order and used as a lodge; the main arena would have been used as a ballroom or auditorium at this time. In the 1930s, the venue's first heavyweight boxing match was held here. The order sold the building in the 1960s, and the Blue Boxing Ring would soon rise to star-studded fame.

The new owners renovated the building and began to hold regular boxing events. The venue went from strength to strength, hosting international, regional, and state title fights within its 1,350-seat arena. World title fights were also held here by the 1990s, and the venue became an important promoter of female African American boxing. The ring was also featured as a set piece in several blockbuster movies, and over the years, the building has also hosted comedy shows, concerts, and weddings. In the early 2000s, the site was recognized as a Historic Marker of the State.

The venue closed around 2010, reportedly due to tax problems. Despite ambitious plans to convert this place into a hotel, jazz bar, and fitness center, this once glamorous building still lies abandoned. The ever-looming threat of demolition hangs over the place, as it occupies land that some think would be better utilized as a soulless parking garage.

As you enter through the main entrance, the striking blue paint is breathtaking. This prestigious arena has often been called “the last great boxing venue”.

The Blue Boxing Ring opened in the early 1960s. It has been left to decay since around 2010.

This upper floor seating area would be crammed with spectators, leaning over the guard rails as they watched the fight below.

The ring has featured in several blockbuster movies. In the 1990s, the venue hosted several world title fights.

Wooden Rollercoaster

This overgrown wooden rollercoaster was once the star attraction at this former theme park. The park has been disused and falling into disrepair for over a decade.

The theme park had humble beginnings in the 1850s as the town's recreation park and fairgrounds. This venue of merriment was turned into a real amusement park in the 1970s, when rides were brought here from another recently closed park. Despite being nearly destroyed by a hurricane shortly after opening, the park enjoyed many decades of success and is fondly remembered by locals.

This rollercoaster is 65-foot tall at the apex and would have traveled at top speeds of 45 mph. This was a "homemade rollercoaster" constructed out of wood, built and maintained by the owner. The track length was over 2 km long. There was a single train with two cars, which would have held twelve passengers per ride. The ride was originally built in the 1930s and survived unharmed until it was damaged by fire in the 1990s. After several months of closure, and a repair bill of over $500,000, the rollercoaster reopened and remained in service until the park closed seven years later.

The owner decided his attention would be better spent on other endeavors and tried to find a buyer for this site shortly after closing it. Sadly, no one emerged intent on returning the park to working order. Most of the rides were auctioned off shortly after the gates closed for the final time.

The old rollercoaster was once the star attraction of a theme park. Now it is being swallowed by the forest as the years pass by.

This 65-foot tall rollercoaster was built in the 1930s and could reach speeds on of up to 45 mph.

Constructed out of wood, it has a track length of around 2 km. This ride would have been built and maintained by the owner.

The theme park closed in the late 1990s. Most of the other rides have been auctioned off, but sadly no buyer was found for this old wooden rollercoaster.

4

AFTER THE FINAL CURTAIN FALLS

Mosque Theater

The Mosque Theater is a stunning example of a Shriner's Temple, built in a lavish Moorish revival architectural style. The building was constructed in the early twentieth century and its four towering minarets saw it become an iconic part of the city skyline.

In the 1930s, the original floor plan was replaced with a sloped floor and fitted with two-tier auditorium-style seating. A stage was added at the front of the temple, and the building was then used as a performing arts theater for much of the twentieth century. The building also continued to host religious rituals and social events for the community.

The ceiling features an iconic stained-glass dome in a vivid array of colors. Typical bold Art Deco-era colors accent the geometric patterns that adorn the proscenium arch above the stage, as well as along the walls of the upper seating level. These are decorative plaster moldings painted vivid burgundy and navy blue, with rich gold paint highlighting the embossed areas of the decorations. Above the stage, there are Arabic-themed scenes, featuring images of camels, bustling marketplaces, and desert dwellings.

As newer and better-equipped theaters began to arrive in town, the theater was forced to close. New owners bought the site at the turn of the twenty-first century, with grand plans to revitalize the building. Essential roof repairs were done to prevent a catastrophic collapse of the domed roof; a roof failure would have been the cue for demolition orders and the loss of this historic building. A financial crisis forced the owners to abandon restoration work. Yet there is hope for this wonderful building as a new restoration project is working in partnership with the local community to offer it a new lease of life.

Above: The Mosque Theater was built in the 1920s, in a lavish Moorish revival architectural style.

Below: The only natural light inside the theater enters through the stained-glass dome skylight. All other windows have been boarded up.

Veronica's Veil

Veronica's Veil is an abandoned theater auditorium in a former Catholic high school. The nearby church and rectory, now converted to condominiums, date back to the mid-1800s. The school buildings were built in the 1880s and enlarged in the 1900s, when this auditorium was added.

The school held one of the longest-running Passion of Christ plays, titled *Veronica's Veil*, which was first performed thirteen years after the auditorium was built. *Veronica's Veil* is an American theatrical adaptation of the end of Christ's life, covering his death and rebirth. The play was very popular in the 1920s, when the auditorium was enlarged to accommodate 800 seats. At this time, the performances, typically held during Lent, drew over 20,000 patrons a year over twenty or more performances.

The church and rectory were sold and redeveloped in the early 2000s, and a local theater group acquired the school and continued performances for several years. However, the play had lost popularity; instead of playing to a packed auditorium, attendance had fallen to less than 4,000 annually. The theatrical group began to struggle financially. Unpaid bills of over $40,000 led to the gas supply to the building being cut. Yet while the group carried on performing, using space heaters to heat the huge hall, audience members began to leave mid-performance.

Theatergoers had to climb thirty-four steps to reach the auditorium, and there were cries for an elevator, citing the Americans with Disabilities Act, to assist entry for disabled customers. The theater group could not afford this, alienating many of the senior citizens, who were some of the group's biggest supporters. Community events and cocktail parties were held in an attempt to raise money for maintenance and modernization of the theater. Attendance levels continued to drop, and by the early 2010s, this once-popular stage saw its final performance.

The building now lies in ruins, floors collapsing and anything of value ransacked years ago. The windows are smashed, and graffiti emblazons the walls.

Above: Veronica's Veil is an abandoned theater auditorium. The building has suffered natural decay but has also been a victim of heavy vandalism.

Below: Even through the decay, a glimpse of the former beauty of this auditorium still manages to shine through.

5

THE GOLDEN AGE OF TRANSPORT

VW BEETLE GRAVEYARD

Deep in the Pennsylvania woods lies an abandoned VW Beetle graveyard. Hundreds of Volkswagen Beetles and Bus Campervans are organized into rows and clusters, seemingly based on age and model. It seems likely this was a junkyard specializing in the German-built bugs and buses, but the business must have ceased trading some years ago. Every color seems represented in this rusting rainbow-colored fleet.

Most of the cars remain complete, missing only a few parts that have presumably been cannibalized for spares over the years. There are also piles of doors, organized by model and neatly arranged into rows leaning against trees. As well as VW Beetles and VW Campervans, there are also several VW Golfs, including a Rabbit LS model from the early 1980s.

One interesting car is painted in an imposing grey and features an aggressive looking grill that may have be sourced from a Rolls-Royce. Careful examination of the headlights and the rear wheel arch suggest this is nothing more than a VW Beetle with an aftermarket kit. These heavily customized fiberglass body kits were popular among enthusiasts in the U.S. and U.K.

There is Mercedes-Benz W114 280, sitting nearby the custom grey Beetle. This appears to be a post-1974 model, with the larger bumper for the American market, which was added to these later models.

There are also several Volkswagen Karmann Ghia, in ivory and brown paint jobs. These cars are essentially a Type 1 Beetle chassis and mechanicals with body styling by Italian designers Carrozzeria Ghia. They were hand built by the German coachbuilders, Karmann. These appear to be late 1960s to early 1970s models, judging by the size of the taillights and the smaller bumper size.

This VW graveyard lays hidden in the woods of Pennsylvania. These brightly colored bugs and buses span the entire color spectrum.

This appears to be a Mercedes-Benz W114 280. The shape and size of the bumper suggest it is a post-1974 model.

There are seemingly endless rows of Volkswagen Beetles and Bus Campervans.

Spare parts are crammed inside some of the VW Campervans, which is a rather inventive and organized storage system.

A particularly interesting VW Beetle has been painted beautiful apple green and features a hand-painted advertisement for an old drug store on its doors.

This collection of red VW Beetles overlooks their brightly-colored relatives in the forest clearing below.

It seems likely this was a junkyard specializing in the German-built bugs and buses, but the business must have ceased trading some years ago.

Many of the cars have been cannibalized for parts over the years; this one is at least missing tires and the original VW logo badges.

There are several Volkswagen Karmann Ghia. These are Type 1 Beetles with body styling by Italian designers that were hand-built in Germany.

The sea of polychromatic cars stretches as far as the eye can see, often packed nose-to-tail in seemingly ordered rows.

Some of the cars are nestled in a shady corner, surrounded by pine trees. Years of pine needles have piled up on the hood, and green mold has grown on the paintwork.

Although most of the cars are Volkswagen, there are some examples of other vehicles and 4 × 4 vehicles.

Despite its initial appearance, this car is a VW Beetle. The previous owner has fitted a fiberglass aftermarket body kit, along with an imposing grille reminiscent of a vintage Rolls-Royce.

This beautiful vintage hood ornament was likely sourced from a 1930s–1950s American car and added to an already heavily customized VW Beetle.

One car is already loaded onto a trailer; perhaps it was a recent arrival or was destined to be taken to a new home just before this junkyard closed.

This ivory and brown Volkswagen Karmann Ghia has a spare tire mounted on the trunk. This was not a standard feature of these 1960s and 1970s vehicles.

This red VW Golf is a Rabbit LS model, dating to the early 1980s.

There are also piles of doors, organized by model and neatly arranged into rows leaning against trees.

Trolley Car Graveyard

Outside of a small town in Pennsylvania, a vintage trolley car graveyard lies hidden in the woods. This rusting collection of treasures from a by-gone age wait patiently for restoration. As the decades roll by, and spray-can wielding teenagers tag the carriages, it seems increasingly likely this forested track will remain their final resting place. A pothole-ridden dirt track leads to the trolleys, which are stored in an area that used to be part of a firm that repaired coal carriages.

A retired Army engineer, a local man, owns these trolley cars. He acquired his first streetcar over thirty years ago, and his collection has been growing ever since. As these trolley cars became available from various cities across America, he snapped them up in order to preserve them for future generations. A lot of cars came from transport companies in Ohio and Pennsylvania: Philadelphia Suburban Transportation, Greater Cleveland Regional Transit Authority, Southeastern Pennsylvania Transportation Authority, and Port Authority Transit of Pittsburgh. Some have been brought here from further afield, including Boston and Kansas City. The owner of these wonderful examples of vintage Americana transportation hopes that one day the right buyer(s) will come and restore these cars to their former glory.

Most of the street cars date back to the 1930s and early 1950s. They were built in the popular, streamlined Art Deco style of the time. Public transport and automobiles were given these sleek shapes and bold designs, to reflect the futuristic wonder of technological advances made at this time.

The most common car types were built by the St. Louis Car Company; there are also numerous examples of Pullman-Standard postwar-style streetcars. There are more modern St. Louis Car Company rapid transit cars, built in the 1980s and 1990s. Several trolley cars lie on their sides, where their wheels and axels have been removed and used to restore active carriages elsewhere. These specimens were too far gone for restoration, so they serve as donors to maintain other cars both within this trolley car graveyard as well as those still in service.

These vintage trolley cars are unusual rusting relics of a bygone age.

Sadly, these trolley cars have been daubed with graffiti over recent years.

Several carriages have been cannibalized for spare parts. These wheels and axels will now be fitted to an active trolley car elsewhere.

Inside the carriages, the original seats and décor appear to have escaped much of the graffiti that "decorates" the outside of the trolley cars.

Above: St. Louis Car Company cars and Pullman-Standard postwar-style streetcars are the most common specimens in this rusty collection.

Below left: The floors of some of the cars have buckled over the years, pushing the seats up or tilted them over.

Below right: A lot of cars came from transport companies in Ohio and Pennsylvania. They are stored in an area that used to be part of a firm that repaired coal carriages.

This collection of treasures await restoration. Hopefully, this forested track will not be their final destination.

The trolley cars were repainted over the years. Here, the original turquoise paint can be seen, as a more recent maroon paint job is flaking away.

Abandoned Steam Locomotive

This old steam locomotive is stored at a car impound after being bought by the present owner in the 1980s. The train was brought to the site on the nearby main railway line and transferred to a warehouse at this impound via a purpose-built temporary railway track.

Over the next few years, it was partially restored, the boiler was repaired, and the engine was steam tested. However, excursions were never run as the running gear system was not repaired or serviced and without the proper legal safety certification, the train was prohibited from moving. At some point, the steam locomotive was moved outside, likely around the mid-2000s. It is becoming increasingly difficult to get a steam engine certified; the skills and knowledge needed are being lost over the years. Those who are still able to perform the certification tests often insist on a full engine rebuild. The locomotive awaits an uncertain future, unable to move under her own steam.

This engine was built in the 1940s by a local locomotive builder. It is a standard gauge 2-10-4-wheel engine; it has two leading wheels on one axle, ten coupled driving wheels, and four trailing wheels in a bogie. These are referred to as "Texas-type" locomotives. During World War II, diesel-powered locomotives began to overtake steam-power in popularity. The newer generation of trains required less maintenance and less personnel to operate, making them more cost effective than steam. The company that built this locomotive closed its doors in the 1950s, after failed attempts to diversify into diesel and electric locomotives.

The locomotive weighs around 520 lb. The coal-fired boiler ran at 250 psi and was rated with a tractive effort of 97,000 lb. A trailing truck booster provided additional weight, upping the total tractive effort to nearly 110,000 lb. The cylinders, which drove the wheels, were 31 inches by 32 inches.

This engine was bought by the present owner in the 1980s and is presently stored on the land behind a car impound.

This engine was built in the 1940s by a local locomotive builder. It is a standard gauge 2-10-4-wheel engine; it has two leading wheels on one axle, ten coupled driving wheels, and four trailing wheels in a bogie.

The locomotive weighs around 520 lb and was powered by a coal-fired boiler.

The train would have arrived on the nearby main railway line, back when it was able to move under its own steam. The owner built a temporary railway track in order to transfer the engine onto his land.

Left: The manufacturer of this engine closed in the 1950s. They had tried (and failed) to diversify into diesel and electric locomotives.

Below: This old steam train became redundant, falling by the wayside as technology progressed. Newer generation diesel trains were cheaper and easier to operate, making them a more cost-effective option.

6

DECLINING EDUCATION

Industrial Trade School

This Industrial Trade School was founded in the early 1900s by an American steel magnate. It was believed that from schools such as these, future captains of industry and innovation would spring. At the dedication ceremony, all local businesses closed for the day, and the town was decorated with bunting. The joyous parades are said to have included over 20,000 people. The local area began to decline in the 1970s and 1980s, and it is likely this school closed soon after the nearby industry collapsed.

This manual training school was well-equipped and offered training as part of local public and church-run school programs. Sixth to eighth grade children were given half-day lessons and practical sessions once a week. High school students typically had a full day at the industrial trade school.

Boys were trained in various handcrafts, such as woodwork and metalwork. The carpentry shop hummed with woodwork machinery, machine rooms were filled with noisy lathes and the blacksmith's forge echoed with clattering anvils. The goal was to train boys in furniture making and to give them some basic trade skills to increase their employment options. They also got to keep the creations they made in class.

There were cooking and sewing classes for girls, in the form of both theory and practical lessons. Girls were taught how to cook both simple and elaborate meals, as well as how to correctly lay a dinner table and how to wait on guests. They were also taught how to be competent seamstresses in the sewing shop. The aim was to prepare girls for married life, tailoring their husband's clothes and cooking the family meals. There were also art rooms for instruction on water-color painting.

There was a top floor auditorium with 700 chairs and a stage. This room was used for local school meetings and high school annual events. Another large room on the upper floor was used as a basketball court, but it is unclear whether these fixtures are a more recent addition.

Sinks such as these are found in several rooms; they were operated by pressing your foot on a metal bar where the sink meets the floor.

The ravages of time can be seen to have taken their toll on this emerald green paint, which is now flaking off from the walls.

The central stairway is painted a beautiful cobalt blue with wrought ironwork featuring Art Deco-style detailing.

Although decay is setting in and paint is peeling off the walls and ceiling, the building appears to be structurally very sound. Perhaps, it can be renovated and brought back into use.

Above: Boys were trained in woodwork and metalwork. Rooms such as this were once filled with machinery and tools. There were cooking and sewing classes for girls. The thrum of sewing machines working in unison would once fill the rooms and corridors.

Below: These trade schools were established to teach boys necessary trade skills, and to prepare them for life in industry. Girls were taught skills deemed fitting for life as a housewife.

There was a top floor auditorium with 700 chairs and a stage. This room was used for local school meetings and high school annual events.

Also on the top floor is a large room that was used as a basketball court, but it is unclear whether these fixtures are a more recent addition.

Trade School Auditorium

This disused Trade School Auditorium was once part of a large vocational training school. The dramatic Art Deco and Classical Revival building is perched high on a hill overlooking the city below. This location was above much of the air pollution produced by the city's steel mills and heavy industry below. The school was built around 1930, costing over $1.5 million.

Some 1,500-1,800 students a year attended this well-appointed school, with classes running both day and night in order to meet the students' needs. There were around thirty workshops, enabling practical training in a variety of skilled trades. Classes would include carpentry, bricklaying, plastering, plumbing, masonry, automobile mechanics, and electrical wiring.

The trade school evolved with the decades, providing relevant education programs to the local workforce. In the 1950s, agriculture was added to the training options. By the 1990s, the school was offering classes in computer technology, literacy, and medical skills alongside the more traditional vocational curriculum.

Sadly, a progressive and constantly updated roster was not enough to save the school. The local manufacturing and industrial sectors steeply declined in the 1990s. As the workforce left the city en-masse in search of better prospects elsewhere, attendance at the trade school plummeted. In the final year of operation, there were around 700 students (way below economic operating capacity). There were also extensive budget cuts in the 1990s, the final nail in the coffin for this once prestigious establishment. The school was forced to close in the mid-2000s.

Over a decade later, the building reopened. This latest incarnation serves as a business center, promoting and fostering green energy research and sustainable practices. Collaboration projects with local universities and colleges, as well as workforce development and training programs, are hosted here. The renovation of the trade school also provided an exemplary case study for sustainable rejuvenation of an older building. The deconstruction and salvage of the old building was carefully planned, with a focus on minimizing the carbon footprint. This old lecture theater lies disused, gathering dust behind closed doors.

This auditorium was once part of a large vocational training school, which was established in the 1930s.

The Trade School provided education and training to the local workforce. Over the decades, the classes evolved to reflect changes in technology and employment trends.

Above: This large auditorium was once filled with students. Now, dust gathers on the chairs and stage.

Below: As the local manufacturing and industrial sectors collapsed in the 1990s, this trade school was left without purpose. With no local employment opportunities, the school closed in the mid-2000s.

Elementary School "L"

Elementary School "L" was built in the early 1900s, with the oldest block being constructed in Classical Revival style. Art Deco stone panels stand proudly above the main entrance. The building was added to the city historic register in the 1980s. Based on available information, it appears the school closed in the mid- to late 2000s.

These buildings started life as a mainstream elementary school, before changing to an "achievement center" offering support to students who did not respond well to more traditional schooling. There was a strong focus on reducing absences, offering support to grades eight through twelve. There were catch-up classes for over-age students, as well as childcare programs supporting young parents as they continued their school education.

The school is remarkably well-preserved and almost entirely free of graffiti. There are many long, dark corridors lined with grey or blue lockers. Numerous classrooms lead off from these corridors; most are bare and relatively unphotogenic. On the lower floors, peeling paint hangs from the ceilings and lies scattered on the linoleum floor.

There is a gymnasium with basketball court markings, complete with a lonely basketball sitting near the middle of the sprung wooden floor.

There is also a moderately-sized auditorium. A painted countryside backdrop hangs to the rear of the stage, a relic of one of the last drama performances nearly a decade ago.

This elementary school closed in the mid- to late 2000s, and now, the corridors lay silent and dark.

This school was an "achievement center"; it offered classes and support tailored to children who did not respond well to mainstream schooling.

A lonely basketball site near the middle of the sprung wooden floor, in the old gymnasium.

The auditorium has a small stage, overlooking rows of long-empty folding chairs.

Above: On the rear wall of the stage, hangs a painted countryside backdrop. Perhaps this was a prop from the final performance.

Below: Paint peels or flakes away onto the floor on the lower levels, littering the dark linoleum.

College Founder's Archive

The College Founder's Archive was built in the mid-1800s by a French American immigrant tycoon and philanthropist. This collection documents the finances of his empire in meticulous detail, spanning over fifty years of trading.

Upon his death, his entire fortune was entrusted to the city. $2 million of his fortune went into building this school, which was intended to provide education for poor orphans. It was originally stipulated in his long and exacting will that the school must only induct "white males." It took over 130 years before social and legal changes finally forced the inclusion of girls, as well as removing the now illegal racial exclusivity. Today, African American students make up 90 percent of the student population.

This building sits at the heart of an active college, the entire campus enclosed by an imposing 10-foot-high wall. This particular building features Greek Revival and Neoclassical architecture. The specific room of interest lies on the third floor.

This room, along with the rest of the building, was intended for classroom use. The large echoing halls and general layout of this building made it a poor lecture venue, and now it houses historically important administration archives of the founder's businesses. He was a fanatical record keeper, documenting all his transactions and flow of wealth in countless ledgers and files. Many of these are stored in large trunks, numbered and dated in his scrupulous fashion. There are also large dusty museum-grade geological specimens tucked away, likely part of the college founders' personal collections.

Above: This room was intended to be a classroom. However, the echoing acoustics and poor accessibility meant it was earmarked as a storage room.

Opposite above: This college was built in the mid-1800s. This collection of documents represents the meticulously cataloged finances of the founder.

Opposite below: The ceiling of the room is domed with a large skylight, which light pours in through.

Above: The bookcases are covered with dust sheets to protect the ledgers and files, some of which are 200 years old. All of the drawers are carefully labeled and numbered.

Opposite above: The rest of this building features Greek Revival and Neoclassical architecture. This landing area connects the third-floor document storeroom to the main stairway.

Opposite below: Tucked away in drawers and hiding under plastic dust sheets are museum-grade fossil and rock specimens.

-1897-
Requisitions on
Matron's Store room
Steward's " "
Requisitions covered
by orders

ABOUT THE AUTHOR

Janine Pendleton has been exploring lost treasures and forgotten places for five years. An impromptu excursion to an abandoned theme park at sunset was the trigger, sparking a fascination in all things derelict. She travels the world in search of abandonment and deterioration, to document what is left behind when people move on. Based in England, she regularly explores the U.K. and Europe in order to capture the hidden beauty in decay. In half a decade, she has explored derelict places in over seventeen countries in constant search of strange and unusual places lost in time. www.obsidianurbexphotography.com